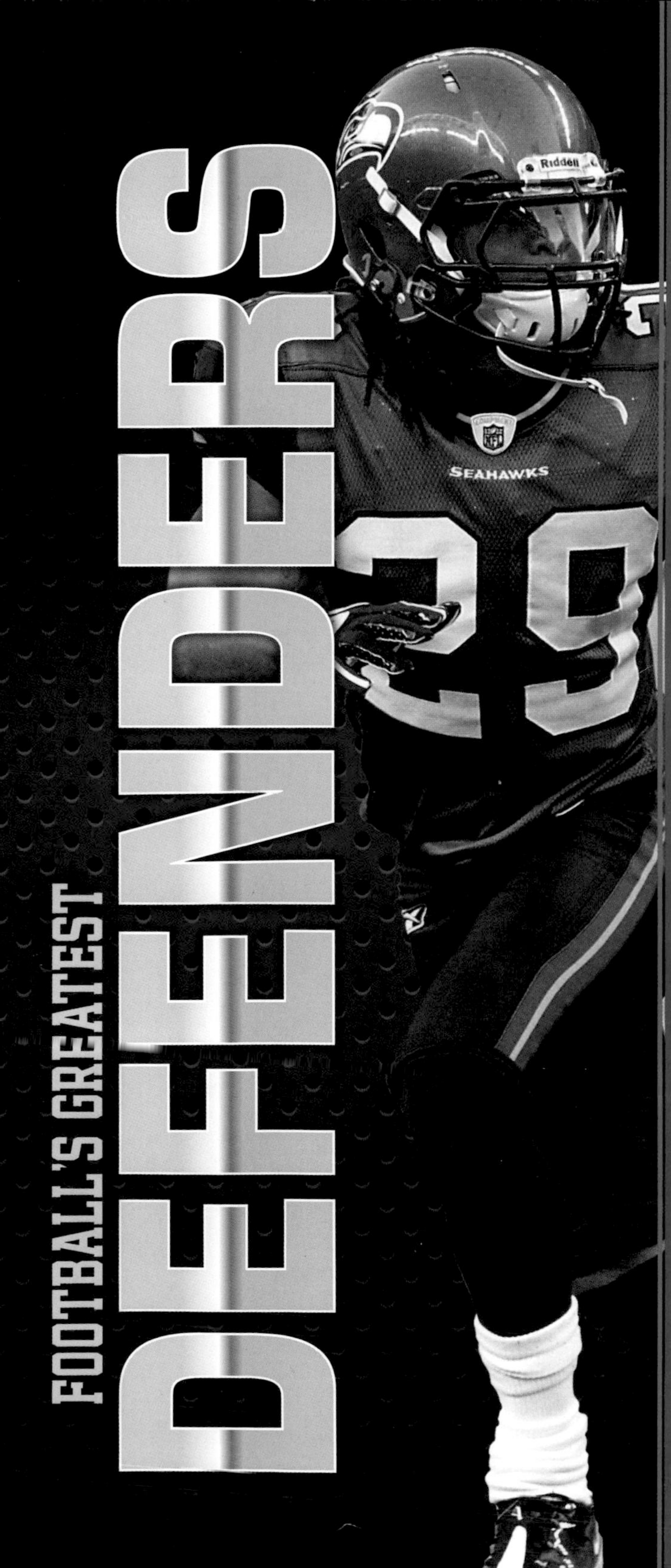

FOOTBALL'S GREATEST DEFENDERS

Sports Illustrated KIDS

BY MATT DOEDEN

CAPSTONE PRESS
a capstone imprint

Sports Illustrated Kids Football's Greatest are published by Capstone Press,
1710 Roe Crest Drive, North Mankato, Minnesota 56003
www.capstonepub.com

Library of Congress Cataloging-in-Publication Data
Cataloging information on file with the Library of Congress
ISBN 978-1-4914-0761-5 (library binding)

Editorial Credits
Brenda Haugen, editor; Heidi Thompson, designer; Eric Gohl, media researcher;
Gene Bentdahl, production specialist

Photo Credits
Getty Images: Joe Robbins, 4t; Newscom: Icon SMI/Jim Dedmon, 11, Icon SMI/MSA, 20, Icon SMI/Ric Tapia, 9, 28, ZUMA Press/Daniel Wallace, 8r, ZUMA Press/Paul Kitagaki Jr., 8l, ZUMA Press/Richard Graulich, 21; Sports Illustrated: Al Tielemans, 5t, 10, 14r, Bob Rosato, 4b, 22, Damian Strohmeyer, 6t, 14l, David E. Klutho, cover, 24bl, 25, John Biever, 5b, 7, 19, John W. McDonough, 6b, 12bl, 15, 24br, 29r, Peter Read Miller, 1, 17, 27l, 27r, 29l, Robert Beck, 12t, 12br, 13, 16, 23, Simon Bruty, 18t, 18b, 24t, 26

Printed in China by Nordica
0414/CA21400595
032014 008095NORDF14

Table of Contents

*All statistics are through the 2013 season.

GENO ATKINS

Cincinnati Bengals defensive tackle Geno Atkins was ready to charge in a 2012 game against the Pittsburgh Steelers. The Steelers were in a passing situation, and the defense knew it. Atkins used a speed rush to blow past his blocker. Then he crashed into quarterback Ben Roethlisberger, dragging him to the ground for a loss of seven yards. Atkins' big hit set the tone in a key Bengals' victory.

Year	Team	Games	Sacks	Tackles
2010	CIN	16	3.0	10
2011	CIN	16	7.5	29
2012	CIN	16	12.5	39
2013	CIN	9	6.0	9

Atkins is smaller than most defensive tackles, but he's one of the best. His high-energy style is what makes him so good. He's constantly moving on the line. His quick feet and surprising power are a rare combination.

Atkins had a great college career at Georgia before entering the 2010 **draft**. But most teams overlooked him because of his small size. The Bengals snapped him up in the fourth round. Atkins has since proven to be the steal of the draft. After serving as a backup for most of 2010, he became a star in 2011. He led the Bengals with 7.5 sacks and made the **Pro Bowl**. In 2012 he tallied 12.5 sacks and was on the **All Pro** First Team. A knee injury sidelined Atkins in early 2013, but not before he was able to tally six sacks. His strong start helped the Bengals reach the playoffs.

draft—the system by which NFL teams select new players
Pro Bowl—the NFL's All-Star Game
All Pro—an honor given to the best NFL player at each position

CLAY MATTHEWS

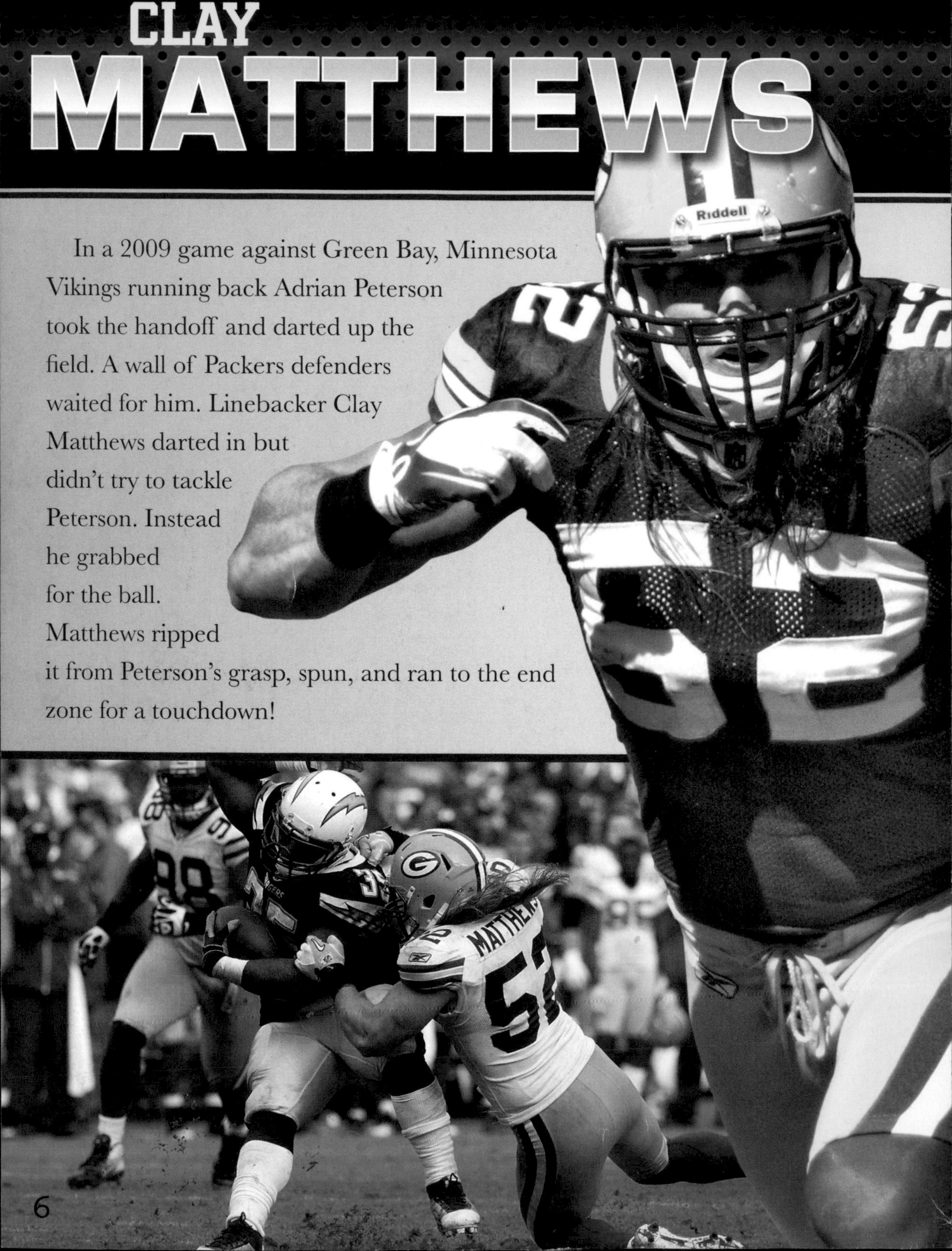

In a 2009 game against Green Bay, Minnesota Vikings running back Adrian Peterson took the handoff and darted up the field. A wall of Packers defenders waited for him. Linebacker Clay Matthews darted in but didn't try to tackle Peterson. Instead he grabbed for the ball. Matthews ripped it from Peterson's grasp, spun, and ran to the end zone for a touchdown!

Matthews' nickname is the Claymaker for a reason. He always seems to be around the ball, ready to make a play. He's strong, smart, and fast. Opposing teams often use two or more men to block him. But even then Matthews finds a way to make a difficult tackle.

Matthews was born into football. His father and uncle both were NFL players. Matthews played football at the University of Southern California. In 2009 the Packers drafted him 26th overall. Matthews was an instant star. Fans loved his hard-hitting style and long, flowing blond hair. Matthews had 10 sacks and made the Pro Bowl as a **rookie**. The next year he helped the Packers win the Super Bowl. The Claymaker has been storming the line ever since.

Year	Team	Games	Sacks	Tackles	Forced Fumbles
2009	GB	16	10.0	36	1
2010	GB	15	13.5	54	2
2011	GB	15	6.0	41	3
2012	GB	12	13.0	32	1
2013	GB	11	7.5	26	3

rookie—a first-year player

PATRICK PETERSON

The Arizona Cardinals and St. Louis Rams were tied in overtime of a 2011 game. St. Louis kicked a booming punt to the Cardinals' one-yard line. Star cornerback and punt returner Patrick Peterson caught it and took off. He zigged and zagged through Rams defenders. Peterson spun a full circle as he avoided a final tackler. Nobody could catch him! His 99-yard punt return won the game for the Cardinals.

Year	Team	Games	Interceptions	Fumble Recoveries
2011	ARI	16	2	2
2012	ARI	16	7	5
2013	ARI	16	3	2

Peterson is a pure athlete. He can outrun and outjump almost anyone. That helps make him one of the NFL's best **shutdown cornerbacks**. But Peterson can do more than play defense. He's also one of the best punt returners in the league. He can even play wide receiver.

Peterson was an **All-American** at Louisiana State before the Cardinals picked him fifth in the 2011 draft. He had a great rookie year. He returned four punts for touchdowns. He also made the Pro Bowl. He proved even better in 2012. He led the Cardinals with seven interceptions and returned to the Pro Bowl. He showed no signs of slowing in 2013 and scored another Pro Bowl appearance.

shutdown cornerback—a defensive player known for his ability to cover great receivers one-on-one
All-American—an honor given to the best players at each position in college sports

DARRELLE REVIS

New York Jets cornerback Darrelle Revis lined up against star receiver Brandon Marshall of the Miami Dolphins in a 2012 game. Miami led the game 3-0 and was driving for another score. Dolphins quarterback Matt Moore dropped back and fired a pass toward Marshall. But Revis cut under the big receiver and grabbed the ball at his own goal line. Interception! Revis darted down the field, weaving through Miami players for an amazing 100-yard touchdown.

Year	Team	Games	Interceptions	Tackles
2007	NYJ	16	3	74
2008	NYJ	16	5	45
2009	NYJ	16	6	47
2010	NYJ	13	0	26
2011	NYJ	16	4	41
2012	NYJ	2	1	8
2013	TB	16	2	43

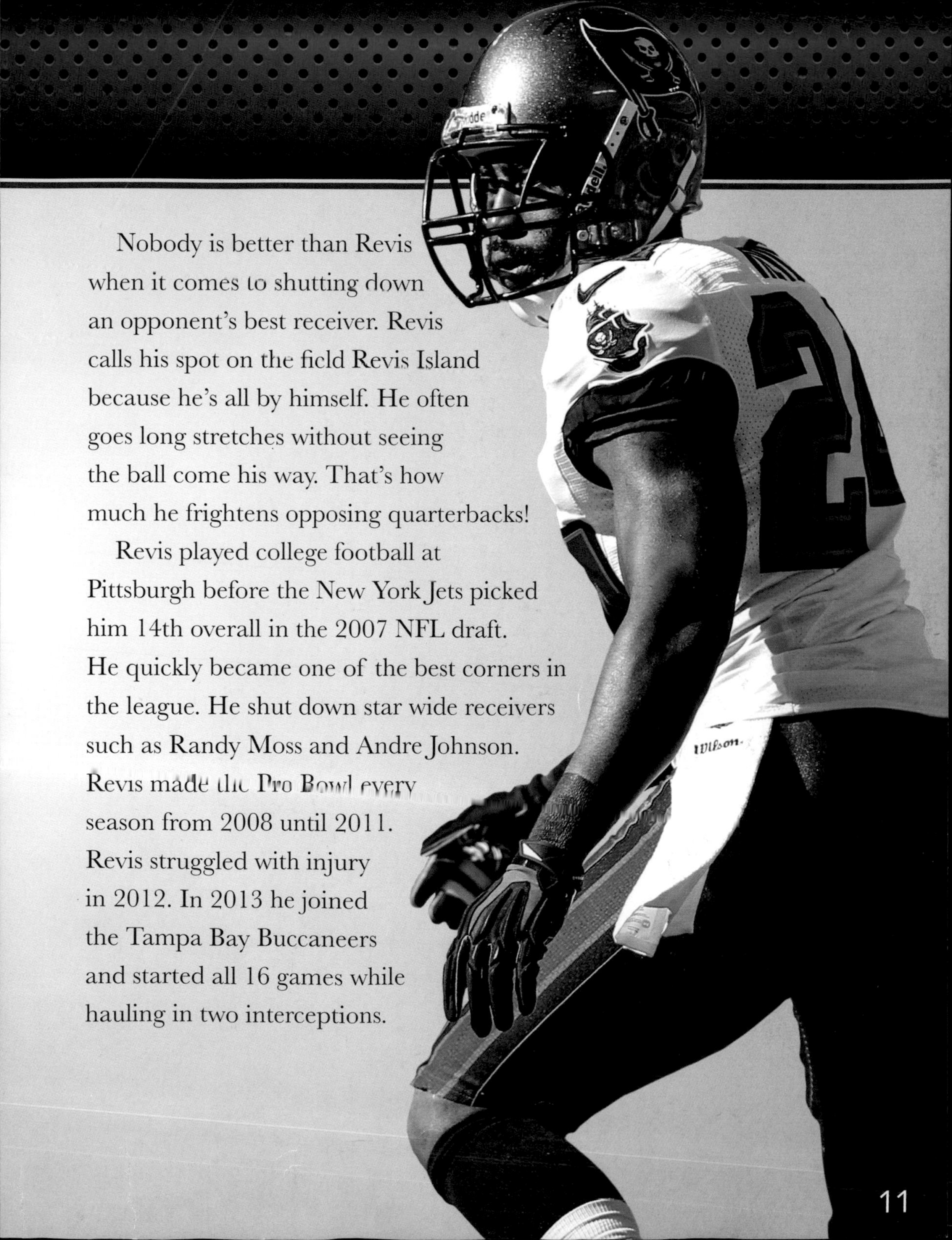

Nobody is better than Revis when it comes to shutting down an opponent's best receiver. Revis calls his spot on the field Revis Island because he's all by himself. He often goes long stretches without seeing the ball come his way. That's how much he frightens opposing quarterbacks!

Revis played college football at Pittsburgh before the New York Jets picked him 14th overall in the 2007 NFL draft. He quickly became one of the best corners in the league. He shut down star wide receivers such as Randy Moss and Andre Johnson. Revis made the Pro Bowl every season from 2008 until 2011. Revis struggled with injury in 2012. In 2013 he joined the Tampa Bay Buccaneers and started all 16 games while hauling in two interceptions.

ALDON SMITH

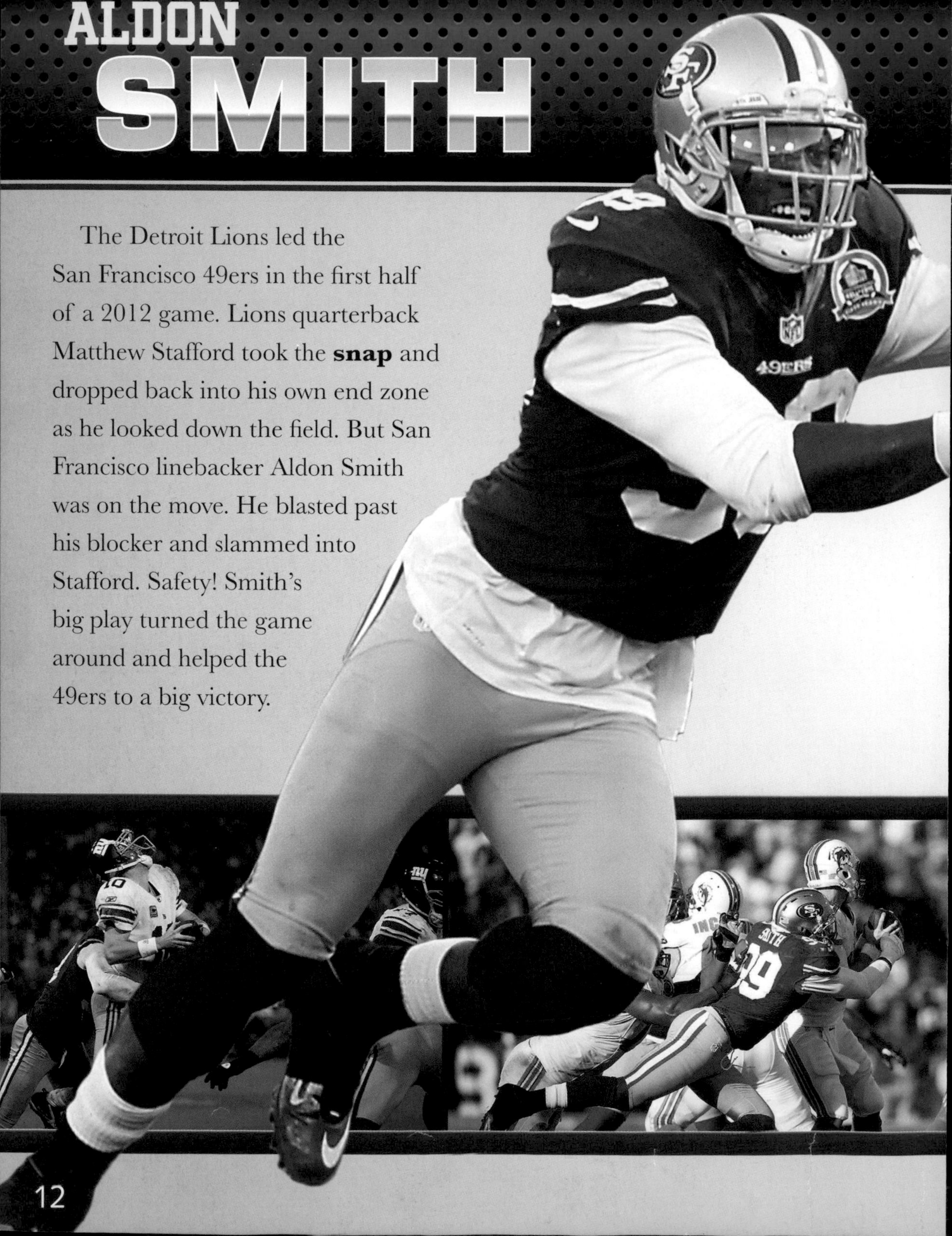

The Detroit Lions led the San Francisco 49ers in the first half of a 2012 game. Lions quarterback Matthew Stafford took the **snap** and dropped back into his own end zone as he looked down the field. But San Francisco linebacker Aldon Smith was on the move. He blasted past his blocker and slammed into Stafford. Safety! Smith's big play turned the game around and helped the 49ers to a big victory.

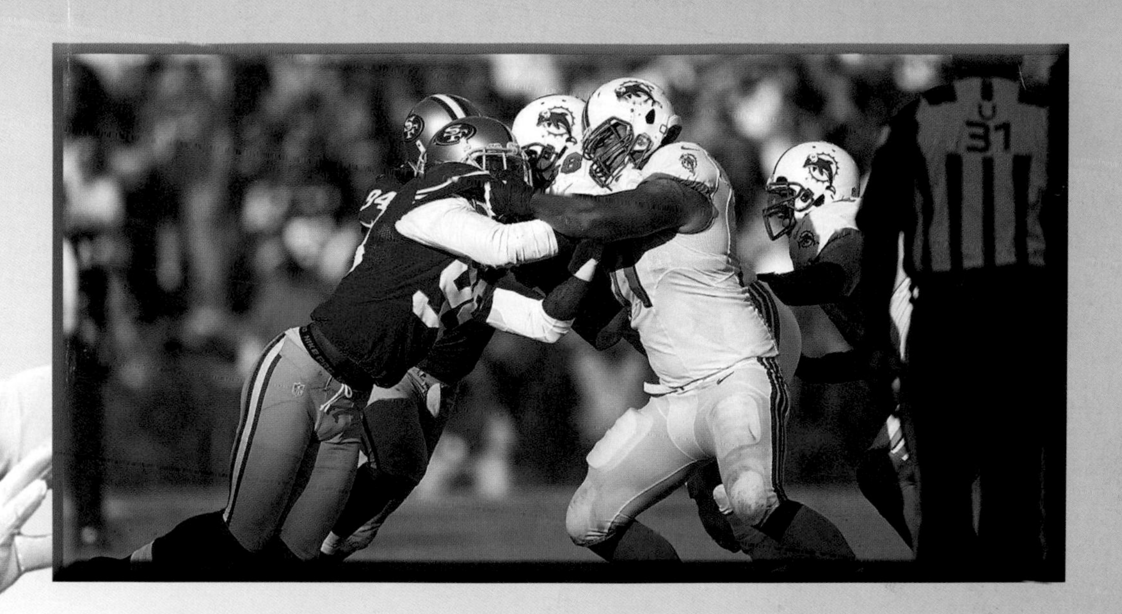

Year	Team	Games	Sacks	Forced Fumbles
2011	SF	16	14.0	2
2012	SF	16	19.5	3
2013	SF	11	8.5	1

Smith is an offensive lineman's worst nightmare. His size and strength let him shrug off blocks. His speed helps him to close in on the quarterback in a heartbeat. His athletic ability allows him to make moves that few players of his size can make.

The 49ers picked Smith seventh overall in the 2011 draft. He didn't start a single game as a rookie, but he still had 14 sacks. Smith moved into the starting lineup and became a dominant pass rusher in 2012. He was second in the NFL with 19.5 sacks, including 5.5 in a single game against the Chicago Bears. Smith was named to the All Pro First Team and was a key part of the defense that led the 49ers to the Super Bowl. Smith had another solid season in 2013 and helped the 49ers nearly reach another Super Bowl.

snap—the act of the center putting the football in play from the line of scrimmage

TERRELL SUGGS

Terrell Suggs was off with the snap. His Baltimore Ravens were clinging to a lead in the 2010 playoffs against the Kansas City Chiefs. As quarterback Matt Cassel dropped back, Suggs rushed around the outside. He reached out and shoved his blocker out of the way. Suggs twisted and lunged at Cassel, driving him to the ground for a six-yard loss. The big play helped Baltimore win the game.

Year	Team	Games	Sacks	Tackles	Forced Fumbles
2003	BAL	16	12.0	18	5
2004	BAL	16	10.5	46	1
2005	BAL	16	8.0	47	3
2006	BAL	16	9.5	47	3
2007	BAL	16	5.0	52	1
2008	BAL	16	8.0	53	2
2009	BAL	13	4.5	44	1
2010	BAL	16	11.0	53	2
2011	BAL	16	14.0	52	7
2012	BAL	8	2.0	17	0
2013	BAL	16	10.0	47	0

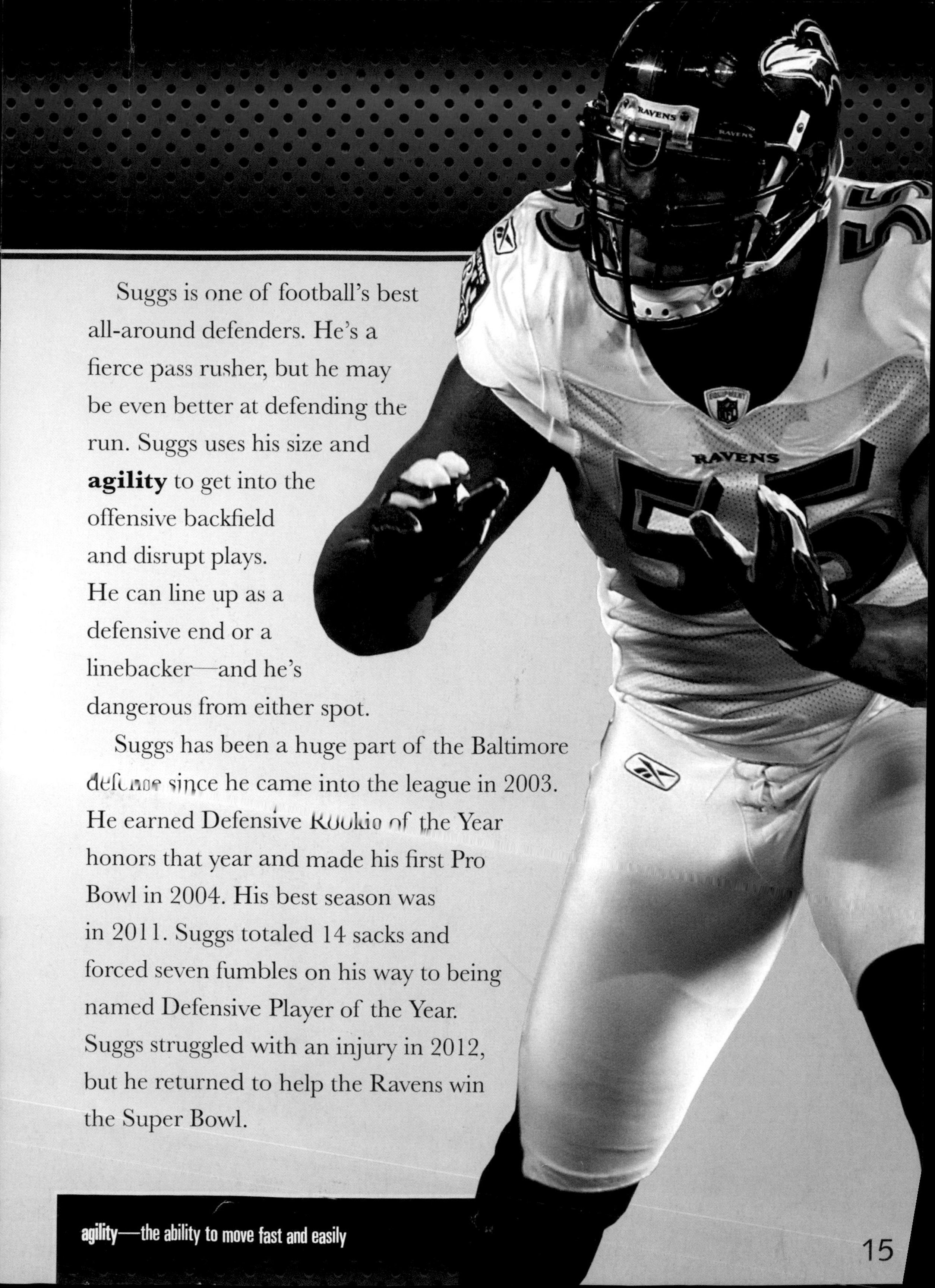

Suggs is one of football's best all-around defenders. He's a fierce pass rusher, but he may be even better at defending the run. Suggs uses his size and **agility** to get into the offensive backfield and disrupt plays. He can line up as a defensive end or a linebacker—and he's dangerous from either spot.

Suggs has been a huge part of the Baltimore defense since he came into the league in 2003. He earned Defensive Rookie of the Year honors that year and made his first Pro Bowl in 2004. His best season was in 2011. Suggs totaled 14 sacks and forced seven fumbles on his way to being named Defensive Player of the Year. Suggs struggled with an injury in 2012, but he returned to help the Ravens win the Super Bowl.

agility—the ability to move fast and easily

EARL THOMAS

Safety Earl Thomas and the Seattle Seahawks were trailing the Atlanta Falcons 27-14 in the fourth quarter of the 2012 playoffs. The Falcons were driving, and a touchdown would put the game out of reach. Atlanta quarterback Matt Ryan heaved a pass downfield. Thomas read the play, sprinted toward the sideline, and snatched the ball out of the air. He tapped his feet down before falling out of bounds. Seahawks' ball! The tide of the game changed, and the Seahawks scored two touchdowns to take a 28-27 lead. Though the Falcons came back with a game-winning field goal, Thomas' interception almost helped turn a blowout loss into a win.

Thomas is one of the smallest players on the field, but his speed and field vision make him a powerful weapon in Seattle's defense. He's just as comfortable coming up to stuff the run as he is dropping back into **coverage.**

Thomas was an All-American in 2009 with Texas. The Seahawks made him the 14th pick of the 2010 draft. Thomas wasted no time impressing Seattle fans. He started all 16 games for Seattle and intercepted two passes in just his third NFL game. Through the years Thomas has only gotten better. He was a Pro Bowler in each of his next three seasons and was named to the All Pro First Team in 2012 and 2013. He helped lead the Seahawks to their first Super Bowl title in 2013.

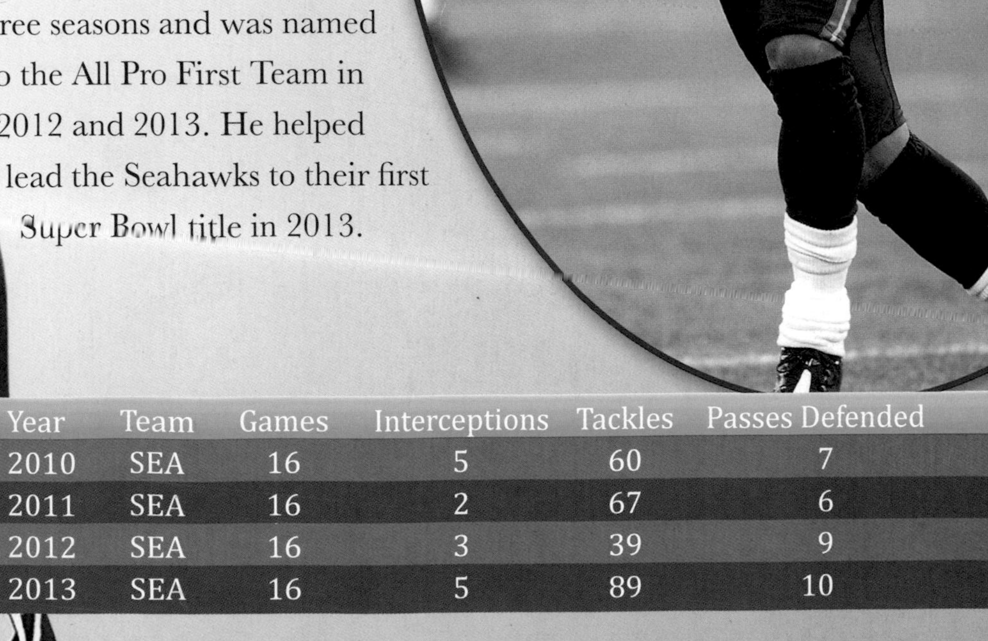

Year	Team	Games	Interceptions	Tackles	Passes Defended
2010	SEA	16	5	60	7
2011	SEA	16	2	67	6
2012	SEA	16	3	39	9
2013	SEA	16	5	89	10

coverage—the setup of defenders covering receivers and trying to stop them from catching passes

CHARLES TILLMAN

The Chicago Bears were playing the Tennessee Titans in a 2012 game, and Charles Tillman was on fire. He already had forced three fumbles in the game. Titans tight end Jared Cook caught a pass and was sprinting down the field. Tillman stepped up and punched the ball out of his hands. It was his fourth forced fumble of the game! No player had ever forced that many in an NFL game since the league began tracking the stat in 1991.

Tillman is the turnover master. Whether he's intercepting passes or forcing fumbles, he always seems to be creating havoc. Tillman's strong hands and great instincts make him one of the best ball-strippers in the NFL.

Tillman was the Bears' second-round pick in the 2003 draft. He wasn't a star right away. But he kept getting better and finally made his first Pro Bowl in 2011. The next year he had an amazing season. He intercepted three passes, forced 10 fumbles, and scored three defensive touchdowns. That performance earned him All Pro honors and another trip to the Pro Bowl. In 2013 Tillman was honored with the NFL's Walter Payton Man of the Year Award.

Year	Team	Games	Interceptions	Forced Fumbles	Defensive TDs
2003	CHI	16	4	2	0
2004	CHI	8	0	1	0
2005	CHI	15	5	4	1
2006	CHI	14	5	1	0
2007	CHI	15	3	3	0
2008	CHI	15	3	4	1
2009	CHI	15	2	4	1
2010	CHI	16	5	4	0
2011	CHI	16	3	4	2
2012	CHI	16	3	10	3
2013	CHI	8	3	3	0

CAMERON WAKE

The Green Bay Packers had the ball in overtime of a 2010 game against the Miami Dolphins. Miami linebacker Cameron Wake was lined up against a rookie offensive lineman. Wake already had two sacks in the game and was looking for number three. As the ball was snapped, Wake tore around the edge, driving his blocker back. Reaching out with one of his long arms, Wake grabbed quarterback Aaron Rodgers and yanked him to the ground for the drive-ending sack. The big play helped spark Miami to a victory.

Year	Team	Games	Sacks	Tackles	Forced Fumbles
2009	MIA	14	5.5	10	1
2010	MIA	16	14.0	48	3
2011	MIA	16	8.5	37	0
2012	MIA	16	15.0	38	3
2013	MIA	15	8.5	28	2

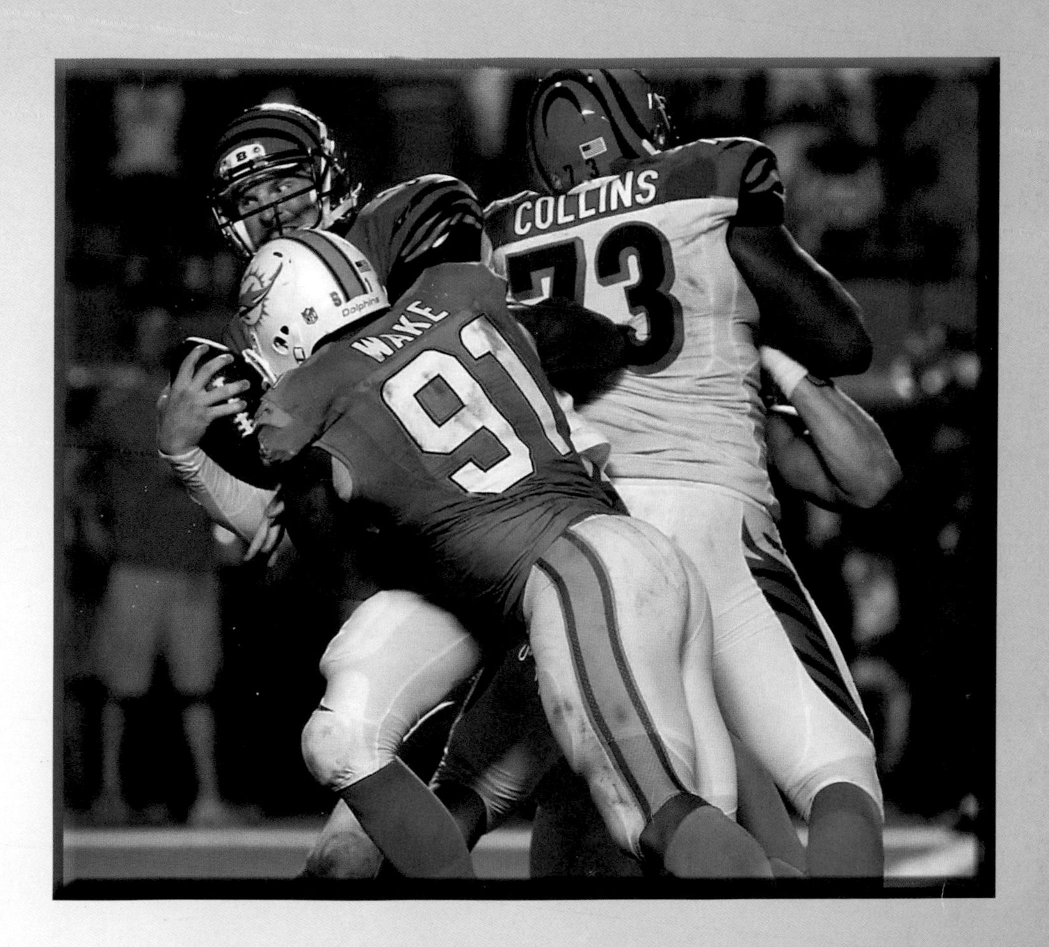

When it comes to elite pass rushers in the NFL, few can stand up to Miami's Cameron Wake. Nobody is better at darting around the edge of the line and chasing down the quarterback.

Wake may be one of the NFL's best now, but that wasn't always the case. Nobody drafted him after he finished college at Penn State. He had to go to the Canadian Football League (CFL) to play. Wake finally got his shot with the Dolphins in 2009. In his first NFL start, he had two sacks and forced a fumble.

Wake started out as a linebacker but switched to defensive end in 2012 and was better than ever. He had 15 sacks and was named to the All Pro First Team. Wake battled a knee injury in 2013 but still earned his third Pro Bowl appearance.

DEMARCUS WARE

New York Giants quarterback Eli Manning took the snap and dropped back in a 2012 game against Dallas. Cowboys linebacker DeMarcus Ware came on a rush. He ducked inside one blocker and then blew past another. Manning avoided one tackler, but he couldn't escape Ware. The Dallas linebacker dragged Manning down for a big loss. It was the 100th sack of Ware's great NFL career.

Year	Team	Games	Sacks	Forced Fumbles
2005	DAL	16	8.0	3
2006	DAL	16	11.5	5
2007	DAL	16	14.0	4
2008	DAL	16	20,0	6
2009	DAL	16	11.0	5
2010	DAL	16	15.5	2
2011	DAL	16	19.5	2
2012	DAL	16	11.5	5
2013	DAL	13	6.0	0

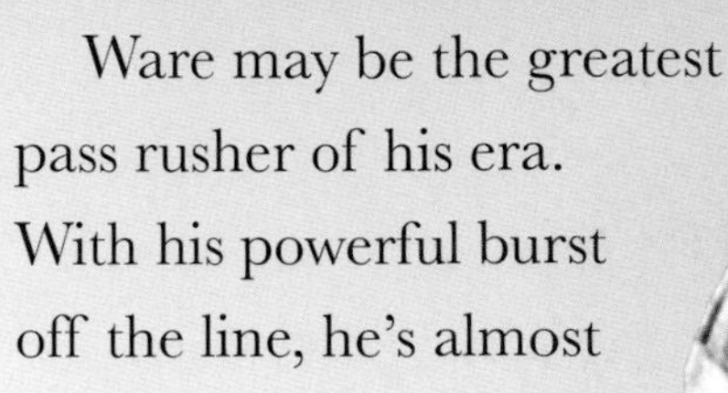

Ware may be the greatest pass rusher of his era. With his powerful burst off the line, he's almost impossible to block with one man. Once he gets the quarterback in his sights, it's all over. Few can escape the quick feet and long arms of the four-time All Pro.

Ware was a college star at Troy before entering the 2005 draft. The Cowboys took him 11th overall. He became a fixture in the Cowboys' defense. Ware didn't miss a single game from 2005 through 2012. He led the NFL in sacks in 2008 and again in 2010. He made his first Pro Bowl in 2006, then returned each of the next six years. Most experts agree that his **durability** and consistent play have made him a lock for football's Hall of Fame.

durability—ability to compete without getting hurt

J.J. WATT

The Houston Texans and Cincinnati Bengals were tied 10-10 late in the first half of a 2011 playoff game. Bengals quarterback Andy Dalton took the snap and dropped back. J.J. Watt battled with an offensive lineman as Dalton fired a quick pass. Watt stood only a few yards away. But he leaped and snatched the ball out of the air. Watt was off to the races, and nobody was going to catch him. Touchdown, Texans! Houston took the lead and never looked back.

Year	Team	Games	Tackles	Sacks	Passes Defended
2011	HOU	16	58	5.5	4
2012	HOU	16	69	20.5	16
2013	HOU	16	65	10.5	7

Houston Texans defensive end J.J. Watt may be the most complete defender in the NFL. His speed, strength, and great footwork make him a pass-rushing beast. But Watt may be even better in coverage. He knocks down more passes than any other defensive lineman in the league.

Watt played college football at Central Michigan and Wisconsin. The Texans picked him 11th overall in the first round of the 2011 NFL draft. Watt started all 16 games for Houston as a rookie. In 2012 he was the NFL's Defensive Player of the Year. Watt led the NFL with 20.5 sacks. He also had 16 passes defended. No other player in NFL history has ever had 15 or more sacks and passes defended in a season.

ERIC WEDDLE

The San Diego Chargers trailed the Cleveland Browns by one point in the fourth quarter of a 2012 game. The Browns had the ball, and Chargers safety Eric Weddle was expecting a running play. He crept up toward the line of **scrimmage** before the snap. Running back Montario Hardesty took the handoff as Weddle sliced in on a **blitz**. He slammed into Hardesty and knocked the ball out of his hands. Hardesty was able to recover it, but the Browns were forced to punt two plays later, giving the Chargers one last chance to take the lead.

Many NFL safeties are good against the pass or the run, but few are truly great against both. Weddle is one of them. He isn't the biggest, strongest, or fastest safety, but he may be the smartest. His ability to read the offense and **anticipate** what's going to happen puts him in the right place to make a play.

Weddle was an All-American at Utah before entering the 2007 draft. The Chargers picked him in the second round. Weddle played safety and also spent time returning punts. In 2011 he really became a star. His seven interceptions led the NFL, and he was named an All Pro for the first time. A solid 2013 season landed him a spot in the Pro Bowl.

Year	Team	Games	Interceptions	Tackles
2007	SD	15	1	42
2008	SD	16	1	103
2009	SD	13	2	68
2010	SD	16	2	79
2011	SD	16	7	66
2012	SD	16	3	83
2013	SD	16	2	94

scrimmage—the imaginary line where a play begins
blitz—play in which a linebacker or defensive back rushes the quarterback
anticipate—to figure out or guess what is about to happen

PATRICK WILLIS

The San Francisco 49ers and Green Bay Packers were tied in the 2012 playoffs. Packers quarterback Aaron Rodgers took the snap. Linebacker Patrick Willis charged on a blitz. As Rodgers scanned the field, Willis blasted past two blockers. He grabbed Rodgers and plowed him to the turf for a nine-yard loss, ending the drive. The 49ers won the game and advanced in the playoffs.

Year	Team	Games	Tackles	Sacks
2007	SF	16	137	4
2008	SF	16	109	1
2009	SF	16	113	4
2010	SF	15	101	6
2011	SF	13	82	2
2012	SF	16	88	0.5
2013	SF	14	100	3

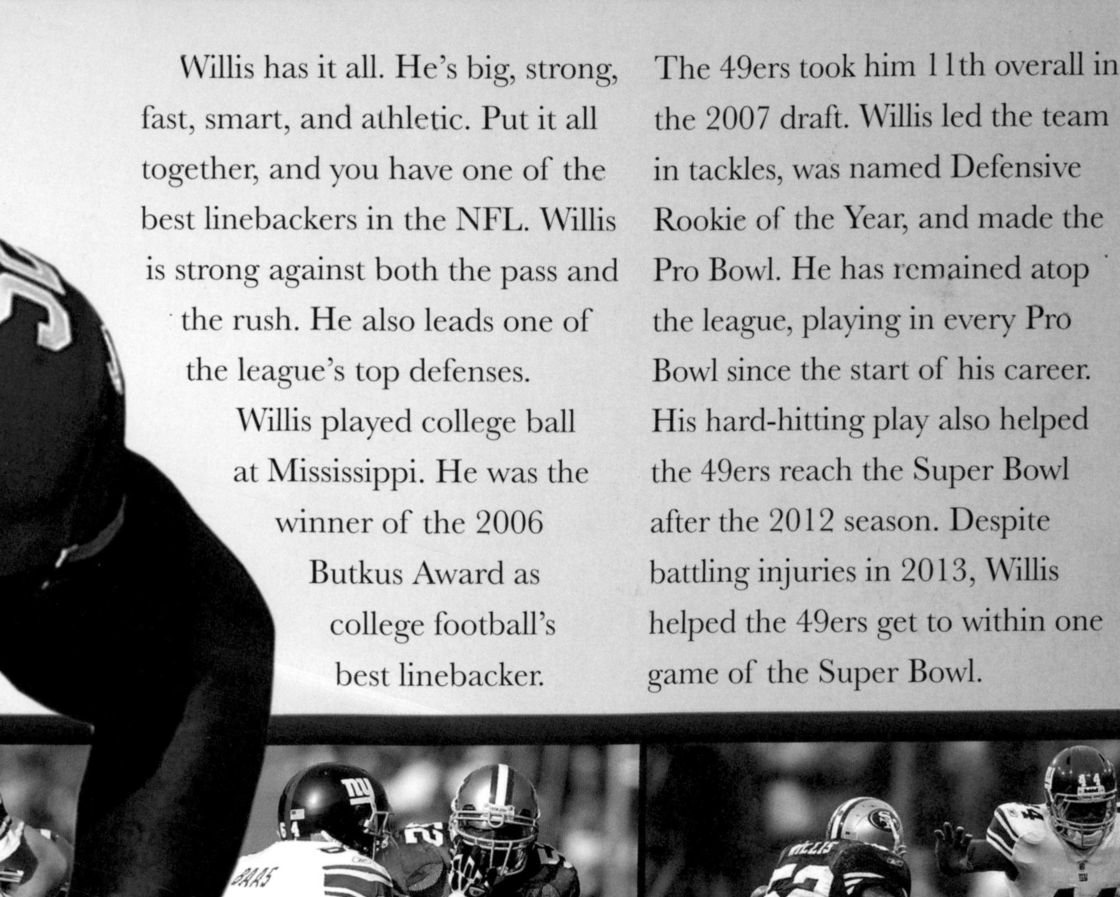

Willis has it all. He's big, strong, fast, smart, and athletic. Put it all together, and you have one of the best linebackers in the NFL. Willis is strong against both the pass and the rush. He also leads one of the league's top defenses.

Willis played college ball at Mississippi. He was the winner of the 2006 Butkus Award as college football's best linebacker. The 49ers took him 11th overall in the 2007 draft. Willis led the team in tackles, was named Defensive Rookie of the Year, and made the Pro Bowl. He has remained atop the league, playing in every Pro Bowl since the start of his career. His hard-hitting play also helped the 49ers reach the Super Bowl after the 2012 season. Despite battling injuries in 2013, Willis helped the 49ers get to within one game of the Super Bowl.

Glossary

agility—the ability to move fast and easily

All-American—an honor given to the best players at each position in college sports

All Pro—an honor given to the best NFL player at each position

anticipate—to figure out or guess what is about to happen

blitz—play in which a linebacker or defensive back rushes the quarterback

coverage—the setup of defenders covering receivers and trying to stop them from catching passes

draft—the system by which NFL teams select new players

durability—ability to compete without getting hurt

Pro Bowl—the NFL's All-Star Game

rookie—a first-year player

scrimmage—the imaginary line where a play begins

shutdown cornerback—a defensive player known for his ability to cover great receivers one-on-one

snap—the act of the center putting the football in play from the line of scrimmage

Read More

Doeden, Matt. *Football Legends in the Making.* North Mankato, Minn.: Capstone Press, 2014.

Polzer, Tim. *Defense!* New York: Scholastic, 2011.

Sandler, Michael. *Pro Football's Stars of the Defense.* New York: Bearport Pub., 2011.

Internet Sites

FactHound offers a safe, fun way to find Internet sites related to this book. All of the sites on FactHound have been researched by our staff.

Here's all you do:

Visit *www.facthound.com*

Type in this code: 9781491407615

Check out projects, games and lots more at **www.capstonekids.com**

Index